BEAUTY AND THE BEAST

**Dramatized
by
William Glennon**

The Dramatic Publishing Company
Woodstock, Illinois • London, England • Melbourne, Australia

*** NOTICE ***

The amateur and stock acting rights to this work are controlled exclusively by THE DRAMATIC PUBLISHING COMPANY without whose permission in writing no performance of it may be given. Royalty fees are given in our current catalogue and are subject to change without notice. Royalty must be paid every time a play is performed whether or not it is presented for profit and whether or not admission is charged. A play is performed anytime it is acted before an audience. All inquiries concerning amateur and stock rights should be addressed to: THE DRAMATIC PUBLISHING COMPANY, 311 Washington St., Woodstock, Illinois 60098.

COPYRIGHT LAW GIVES THE AUTHOR OR HIS AGENT
THE EXCLUSIVE RIGHT TO MAKE COPIES.

This law provides authors with a fair return for their creative efforts. Authors earn their living from the royalties they receive from book sales and from the performance of their work. Conscientious observance of copyright law is not only ethical, it encourages authors to continue their creative work. This work is fully protected by copyright. No alterations, deletions or substitutions may be made in the work without the prior written consent of the publisher. No part of this work may be reproduced or transmitted in any form or by any means, electronic or mechanical, including photocopy, recording, videotape, film, or any information storage and retrieval system, without permission in writing from the publisher. It may not be performed either by professionals or amateurs without payment of royalty. All rights, including but not limited to the professional, motion picture, radio, television, videotape, foreign language, tabloid, recitation, lecturing, publication, and reading are reserved. On all programs this notice should appear: "Produced by special arrangement with THE DRAMATIC PUBLISHING COMPANY of Woodstock, Illinois."

©MCMLXIV by
WILLIAM GLENNON
Revised ©MCMXCI
Printed in the United States of America
All Rights Reserved
(BEAUTY AND THE BEAST)

ISBN 0-87129-053-7

BEAUTY and the BEAST

A Play in Three Acts
For Four Women and Six Men

CHARACTERS

PAULETTE .... sister of Beauty
HENRIETTE .... another sister of Beauty
PAUL .... brother of Beauty
HENRI .... another brother of Beauty
TOOT SWEET .... an old family servant
POPPA .... Beauty's father
THE PAGE .... servant of the prince
THE PRINCE .... who becomes the Beast
THE SPIRIT
BEAUTY

TIME: Long ago.

PLACE: A forest, a cottage and a palace.

SYNOPSIS OF SCENES

ACT ONE
A clearing in the forest. Afternoon.

ACT TWO
The cottage exterior. Six months later.

ACT THREE
Scene One: The interior of the palace. Night.
Scene Two: The interior of the palace. Later.

ACT ONE

AT RISE: *Only the figure of SPIRIT in a flowing gown can be seen somewhere behind a scrim, swaying and moving a bit to mysterious music; as she begins to speak, the music fades under. Her voice, if possible, is miked.*

SPIRIT *(intoning, musically).* A realm of air and trees and flowers...See where you are. A kingdom of space and beauty. Mine and yours and yours and yours. If you dream a dream, dreams come true...

(Music fades out and SPIRIT vanishes as lights come up on stage. It is a lovely forest, almost magical. Voices in the near distance.)

HENRIETTE *(off).* Slow down, Paulette! I can't keep up.
PAULETTE *(off).* No one asked you to keep up, ninny.
HENRIETTE *(off).* You'll be sorry if I get lost! Paulette!

(PAULETTE enters, rather grandly dressed for a country scene. She looks about.)

HENRIETTE *(off).* Better not hide from me, or I'll tell Poppa! Paulette! Answer me!

PAULETTE *(unconcerned).* What a ninny. Hopeless. *(Calls back.)* I'm over here, Henriette. Try using your eyes. And your head.

(HENRIETTE runs on, breathless. She's younger, a little naive but quite nice.)

HENRIETTE. Paulette! Where are you? *(She takes PAULETTE's hand and stares at her.)* Oh, there you are.
PAULETTE. You're a ninny, Henriette. I mustn't forget to tell you.
HENRIETTE. I thought you'd left me alone.
PAULETTE. I did.
HENRIETTE. You did? Why?
PAULETTE. To go exploring. But now I'm bored.
HENRIETTE. I'm hungry. When do we have our picnic?
PAULETTE. Who cares? Go back and ask the others. I despise picnics.
HENRIETTE. Then why'd you agree to come along? Just to please Poppa, I'll bet. So he won't scold you for all those new dresses you ordered.
PAULETTE. Poppa doesn't know about them.
HENRIETTE. Not yet. But he might find out.
PAULETTE. If you dare open your big mouth, I'll stick a bon-bon in it. *(They laugh.)* Then I'll tell Poppa about all the sweets you've been sneaking.

(PAUL and HENRI enter, carrying a wasps' nest on a branch. The young MEN are elegant, accustomed to a life of ease.)

HENRI. Look what we've found!
PAUL. *I* found. It was just hanging on a tree.

Act I   BEAUTY AND THE BEAST   Page 7

PAULETTE. What is it, Paul?
PAUL. I haven't decided.
PAULETTE. Which means you don't know.
HENRIETTE. Let's see. Is it a pear?
HENRI. No, *I* think it's a kind of a seashell.
PAULETTE. In the forest?
HENRI. Well, listen. You can hear a noise inside like the ocean.
PAUL. Sort of a buzzing. *(ALL listen and make buzzing sounds in imitation.)*
HENRIETTE. Maybe it's a coconut.
PAUL. Coconuts don't buzz.
PAULETTE *(grabbing it)*. The buzzing gets louder when you shake it.
HENRI. We'll give it to Poppa, as a gift.
PAUL. Give it to me, I found it. *(Takes it.)*
HENRIETTE. What's this little hole here?
PAUL. Let me see. *(Steps away and puts his finger in the hole.)* I do believe I can feel something moving. *(Screams.)* I've been stung!

(ALL scream as they toss the nest back and forth. It finally goes to the old family servant, TOOT SWEET, on his entrance. He puts the picnic basket down, covers them with a tablecloth as they sit on a log, and gets rid of the nest off stage. They wait for him to uncover them.)

PAUL. Toot Sweet! Look! I've been stung!
TOOT SWEET. Well, who ever heard of playing ball with a wasps' nest?
HENRI. We thought it was a seashell.
HENRIETTE. Or a coconut.

TOOT SWEET *(ripping off a bit of tablecloth or using a hankie.)* Here, Paul, I'll put a bandage on it.

HENRIETTE. Me, too.

TOOT SWEET. Did you get stung?

HENRIETTE. No, but I want a bandage.

PAULETTE. What you really want, Henriette, is a brain.

HENRI. Let me help. *(Twists ends of bandage.)* There!

PAUL *(screams).* Stop it! If I weren't wounded, I'd box your ears.

PAULETTE. That might be amusing.

HENRIETTE. Is that our picnic, Toot Sweet?

TOOT SWEET. Yes, but we'll hold off 'til your sister and poppa join us.

PAULETTE. Where are they, anyway?

HENRI. Fetch them here. Be off with you.

PAUL. And while you're at it, fetch me a doctor.

TOOT SWEET. Pish tosh. *(Turns in time to see HENRIETTE approaching the basket.)* Hands off! *(HENRIETTE retreats.)* Now, wait here like good little children 'til I find Beauty and your father.

PAULETTE. We're not children.

TOOT SWEET. Well, wait anyhow. *(He goes. Pause.)*

HENRIETTE. Little meat pies, probably.

PAULETTE. No, I think it's cold chicken.

HENRI. And grapes.

PAUL. Seedless?

(They start toward the basket. TOOT SWEET is back in a flash.)

TOOT SWEET. I repeat: hands off! *(After a quick hard glare, he goes.)*

PAULETTE. I don't think he trusts us.

Act I   BEAUTY AND THE BEAST   Page 9

PAUL. He's acting awfully bossy these days.

HENRI. He always has. Bossiest servant we've got.

HENRIETTE. I'm still hungry. *(The lights have been dimming a little.)*

PAULETTE. We'd better get this stupid picnic over with before it rains. *(Little pause.)*

SPIRIT *(voice)*. See where you are. My special place. See where you are.

PAULETTE *(as they ALL look around mystified)*. I know where I am, Henriette. I'm out in the woods and I don't much like it.

HENRIETTE. That wasn't me.

SPIRIT *(voice)*. Open your eyes and see where you are.

HENRI *(as they look about)*. Maybe it's Beauty.

PAUL. Does anyone else feel a little funny?

PAULETTE. No. But you look a little funny. You always do.

PAUL. I'll thank you to hold your tongue.

HENRI. Or we'll snip it out.

PAULETTE. Listen to the peacocks.

HENRIETTE. Shh! Everyone listen!

SPIRIT *(voice)*. My realm is here, my kingdom of the spirits is all about...see where you are...

PAULETTE. For heaven's sake, what's Beauty trying to do? Scare us? *(Calling.)* Beauty!

HENRI. That wasn't Beauty.

PAUL. And I do feel funny.

HENRIETTE. Me, too. *(A pause. They are nervous and a little dazed.)*

(TOOT SWEET comes in.)

TOOT SWEET. They're coming. I found them way back by the stream. *(Calls back.)* We're here, Beauty!

HENRIETTE. See. It wasn't Beauty.

TOOT SWEET. What wasn't?

HENRIETTE. The voice, Toot Sweet. The voice we heard. I knew it wasn't Beauty. Didn't fool me for a minute.

PAULETTE. Well, then, who was it?

PAUL. No one.

PAULETTE. How could it be no one? You heard it, too.

PAUL. I don't think I did. So there.

PAULETTE. You've got a small problem, Paul. You're mad.

HENRIETTE. The voice said it was her kingdom or it was a special place or something.

HENRI. It was very weird, very.

TOOT SWEET. Hearing voices, huh? Too much sun. Maybe you're all getting sick.

PAULETTE. And maybe you're getting too pushy.

TOOT SWEET. Fiddle-dee-dee.

(BEAUTY enters, sees them, and the place.)

BEAUTY. I don't believe it! Tell me, how did you find it? I wasn't sure I'd be able to myself.

PAULETTE. Find what?

BEAUTY. The place! The special place I told you about.

HENRI. Aha! It *was* Beauty, see?

PAULETTE. Not if she was back by the stream. How could we hear from that distance? You're all crazy.

BEAUTY. What's the matter?

HENRIETTE. We heard a voice, Beauty.

HENRI. Obviously yours.

Act I   BEAUTY AND THE BEAST   Page 11

HENRIETTE. The voice told us to look out, or open our eyes, stuff like that. Are you sure it wasn't you, Beauty?

BEAUTY. It wasn't. But don't you remember last night, when we planned the picnic...

PAULETTE. *You* planned it, *I* didn't.

BEAUTY. I told you I'd find an extra special place.

PAUL. Which gives me the creeps.

PAULETTE. Which you already had. But that was last night, and we heard the voice just now.

TOOT SWEET. Or thought you did. They're playing one of their games, Beauty. Pay no attention.

PAUL. Games are for children, Toot Sweet.

TOOT SWEET. Like you, Paul.

PAULETTE. It's no game and no fun and I want to go home. Now!

(POPPA enters in time to hear the last.)

POPPA. But, Paulette, dear, we haven't had our picnic yet. And I for one am famished. It's this great country air, I expect.

BEAUTY. And, look Poppa, isn't this the perfect spot?

POPPA. As perfect as these. *(He carries some wild roses.)* See? Wild roses. I found them near the stream.

PAULETTE. I prefer our gardens at home.

POPPA. Nothing there to match these. *(Gives one to BEAUTY.)*

BEAUTY. Thank you, kind sir.

POPPA. A pleasure, madam!

HENRIETTE. What about me?

POPPA. To match the bloom in your cheeks, fair mistress.

(HENRIETTE giggles and takes the rose. To PAUL-

ETTE.) The poor rose pales beside your elegance, great lady, but take it, please, to make me happy.

PAULETTE. Oh, Poppa, you do have a way.

HENRI. So I don't get a present. Do I care? No. Do you, Paul?

PAUL. I could care less.

PAULETTE. Poor babies. *(PAULETTE and HENRIETTE chase BOYS and put the roses in their lapels or hair or behind their ears.)*

TOOT SWEET *(getting at the picnic things).* If you'll stop acting like two-year-olds we'll have our lunch.

PAULETTE. No. For once in his life Paul's right.

PAUL. Mercy!

PAULETTE. This place is too creepy.

BEAUTY. Oh, it is not! It's lovely. Now, listen, I'll tell you something very interesting, if you stay.

PAULETTE. Tell us on the way back, Beauty. We can have luncheon at home.

PAUL. Besides, I need professional attention for my poor finger.

HENRI. I could snip it off at the elbow, if you like.

HENRIETTE. Come on, Beauty, let's go home.

TOOT SWEET *(pleasantly).* We're going to stay right here and have our lunch, whether you like it or not, so you may as well like it.

PAUL. I vote we go home.

HENRI. I second it.

BEAUTY. Not yet, please.

POPPA *(sitting on stump or log).* As a favor to your tired old poppa.

TOOT SWEET. It doesn't make any sense to beg them.

PAULETTE. He's right for once.

Act I BEAUTY AND THE BEAST Page 13

TOOT SWEET. They're children. You don't beg children to do something. You *tell* them. *And I tell you you're staying!*

(ALL react. During the next few lines the PAGE, a young boy, obviously very frightened, runs on silently, sees them and hides.)

PAULETTE. That's the last time he calls us children.
PAUL. You're getting way out of line, Toot Sweet.
HENRI. Poppa, let's go home and leave Toot Sweet here.
PAULETTE. Hopefully to starve.
POPPA. Now, now, now.
BEAUTY. Toot Sweet's right! You're acting like children! *(They react.)* And I'm ashamed of you. Spoiling things for Poppa.
TOOT SWEET. When you hear the news, you'll sing a different tune.
POPPA. Not yet, Toot Sweet.
TOOT SWEET. Sorry. But they'll have to know sometime.
PAULETTE. Know what?
BEAUTY. Know that we've found the perfect spot for our picnic.
PAULETTE. That isn't it. Know what, Toot Sweet? Poppa, are you hiding something? *(Pause.)*
POPPA. What shall we do, Beauty?
BEAUTY. For now, Poppa, smile.
PAULETTE. You're talking in riddles.
PAUL. It's this place, that's part of it.
BEAUTY. Yes, you're right, Paul, this place *is* part of it. Part of what I have to tell you. I thought it would be easier here. *(A pause. They look at each other, wonder-*

ing. BEAUTY looks up, as though she senses something and before they can speak she stops them.) Shh! Listen! *(Pause, the lights change, music is heard.)*

SPIRIT *(voice).* A realm of air and trees and flowers...a kingdom of space and beauty...if you dream a dream, dreams come true...*(The feeling of a spell has been cast.)*

PAULETTE *(not breaking the spell).* That voice, Beauty. Who is it?

BEAUTY. A spirit, I think. A lady. A lady of dreams perhaps. *(Pause.)* Once long ago, when I was just a little girl I wandered off to gather flowers. I think there was a birthday or a party, and I was hoping to find the prettiest blossoms in the world. Well, I went further and further, and then I found them—here. So very beautiful, but I couldn't reach them. They were up too high.

HENRIETTE. What happened?

BEAUTY. I wished, Henriette. I closed my eyes and I wished. *(She closes her eyes.)* Please. Some blossoms for our little party. *(The music rises.)*

SPIRIT *(voice).* Dreams come true...*(And a few blossoms fall from atop the trees. Silence. Astonishment.)*

BEAUTY. Thank you. *(She picks up one, smiles at her FAMILY and they gather the other blossoms and give them to BEAUTY.)* See, Poppa. All is not lost. Dreams can come true.

PAULETTE. If you told me about this I wouldn't believe it.

PAUL. I still don't.

BEAUTY. It's ages since I've been here. Too busy at home. But it's still so dream-like.

HENRIETTE. You mean you didn't keep coming back here and asking for things?

BEAUTY. No.

HENRIETTE. Not even a handsome young prince? *(BEAUTY smiles.)*

HENRI. Why didn't you tell us about it?

BEAUTY. I almost did. Poppa, remember when I gave you the blossoms?

POPPA. Yes. I said, "They're beautiful, Beauty. Where did you find them? In a very special place?"

BEAUTY. And I said, "Very special."

POPPA. "Will you take me there?"

BEAUTY. "Someday, perhaps. But for now it's a secret."

PAULETTE. Then why today?

TOOT SWEET. Because we have need of dreams, Paulette.

BEAUTY. I'll try to explain.

POPPA. It's my responsibility, Beauty, let me try.

PAULETTE. Well, *someone* try, for heaven's sake!

TOOT SWEET *(blurting it out)*. Your poppa's poor, my young lovely. He's lost everything. That's what they're trying to tell you. Houses, gardens, jewels, stables, money, the lot—it's all gone. We're poor as church mice.

POPPA. We still have each other.

BEAUTY. And a little cottage nearby—we're far from poor. *(Pause.)*

PAULETTE. This is going too fast. What are you talking about?

PAUL. It's this creepy place, making them babble nonsense.

POPPA. Not long ago I invested in ships to the Orient.

HENRI. But you've done that before.

POPPA. I know. But these ships were lost in a storm, and I'd invested everything.

HENRIETTE. Everything?

PAULETTE. First we hear voices and now this. It's like a nightmare.

BEAUTY. Toot Sweet...

TOOT SWEET. I didn't mean to blurt it out. Sorry.

PAULETTE. So this is your big surprise.

BEAUTY. I brought you here hoping the spirit would make it easier for me to tell you, easier for you to accept.

PAULETTE. That's it, Beauty! Ask the spirit! No, I will. Listen, spirit, or lady, or whatever, we need more than blossoms, we need our fortune back! That's my dream, hear? *(Pause. Music.)*

SPIRIT *(voice)*. Take care...take care with your dreams... *(A great crash of thunder, music out.)*

PAULETTE *(almost defeated)*. Oh, Beauty. *(She goes and holds her.)* It's terrible. It's just terrible. I don't think I can bear it.

TOOT SWEET *(gently)*. You'll survive.

BEAUTY. You'll do more than survive. You'll find out how strong you really are.

PAULETTE. I don't want to be strong. I want to be rich.

PAUL. Well, I should think so.

HENRI. Being poor just doesn't make sense.

HENRIETTE. I know. What'll I do about my sweet tooth?

POPPA. Children, children, try to forgive me. Please. Things will change before you know it. You'll see. And look, Toot Sweet has agreed to stay on and help us over the rough spots.

BEAUTY. And wait till you see the cottage. It's charming. Like a big dolls' house. *(They groan a little.)* We'll hang on to our dreams, and take care of them, the way the spirit said, and before you know it, there will be blossoms falling for all of us.

SPIRIT *(voice)*. Seek your dreams in your hearts...see what is in your hearts...dreams come true...*(Pause. POPPA rises and holds out his arms. PAULETTE and HENRIETTE are the first to go to him, then PAUL and HENRI. BEAUTY hugs TOOT SWEET before she joins GROUP.)*

POPPA. Well, now.

PAULETTE *(breaking the mood)*. How far away is this big dolls' house?

TOOT SWEET *(smiling)*. A hop, skip and a jump.

PAULETTE. Well, let's hop to it. You two boys and Henriette will have to clean it out before Beauty and Toot Sweet can get dinner. We'll all be quite hungry since we missed lunch. *(They start out.)*

PAUL. And just what do *you* plan to do, Miss High and Mighty?

PAULETTE. Give orders, Paul. Hop! Skip! Jump!

(They have gone, forgetting the basket. In a moment PAGE comes out of hiding, runs to look off after them, then to see in every direction. He is alert and frightened. He goes to the basket and kneels, about to investigate the contents. Upstage, the PRINCE, a handsome, arrogant young man, runs in silently, sees PAGE and stops, and begins to advance stealthily. From his belt he takes a small length of rope. Just as PAGE is about to take some food, PRINCE grabs him from behind. PAGE gasps in fright. Quickly, PRINCE topples PAGE, straddling him while he ties his hands in back.)

PRINCE. So. Our runaway is also a thief.
PAGE. Please, Your Highness. I was...hungry.

PRINCE. Too much exercise. *(Finishes with the rope, and then drags PAGE to his feet.)* Get up. Well. You've given me a merry chase, haven't you? And why, do you suppose the prince himself would run after the likes of you? Well, I'll tell you, boy. I do not intend to have page boys who are trained to serve me escape their duties. Besides, I like the chase. Now, what shall your punishment be?

PAGE. Please, Your Highness, I'm sorry.

PRINCE. Sorry I caught you? Your trail was easy to follow. *(Thunder. PRINCE looks around.)* I thought I heard voices a moment ago.

PAGE. Yes, they're gone. Except for the Spirit.

PRINCE. The what?

PAGE. There's a spirit here, in the trees or somewhere.

PRINCE. What little trick are you playing now?

(PRINCE sees someone coming and grabs PAGE and goes to one side, holding his hand over PAGE's mouth as HENRIETTE enters from the other side.)

HENRIETTE. Aha! I knew it! *(She picks up the picnic basket and starts off, then turns and looks up.)* You looked after it for us, didn't you? That was nice. I promise, Spirit, we'll do just what you said. We'll seek our dreams in our hearts. That *was* it, wasn't it? Got to run, we're all awfully hungry! *(She laughs and goes out. PRINCE cautiously comes back in scene, still holding PAGE.)*

PRINCE. What was that prattle about dreams?

PAGE. I told you—there's a spirit here...

PRINCE *(shoves PAGE away)*. Nonsense!

SPIRIT *(voice)*. Dreams come true...dreams come true...

Act I   BEAUTY AND THE BEAST   Page 19

PRINCE. Who speaks?
PAGE. See?
SPIRIT *(voice)*. A realm of air and trees and flowers...
PRINCE *(looking for her)*. What place is this?
SPIRIT *(voice)*. A kingdom of space and beauty...if you dream a dream...
PRINCE. I claim it in the name of the crown! Look, boy, up there.
PAGE. What is it?
PRINCE. The top of that hill yonder.
SPIRIT *(voice)*. Dreams come true...
PRINCE. Are you a spirit? Can you work magic? Can you make dreams come true? Answer me!
PAGE. Careful, Your Highness.
PRINCE. Quiet. I'll attend to you later. Playing hide and seek all day has paid off. That hill top over there. I kept seeing that spot, from the valleys, from the other hills, through the trees, while I chased you. It's perfect.
PAGE. Perfect for what?
PRINCE. A new palace, greater than any I've ever built! Spirit, hear my dream. A palace, a palace unmatched anywhere, rising on that hill like a great jewel.

(The music rises and we now see SPIRIT.)

PAGE. Look, Your Highness, there she is!
PRINCE *(excited)*. Then it's true! You are a spirit! Did you hear my dream?
SPIRIT. A rising jewel...unmatched anywhere...
PRINCE. Yes, yes, filled with the world's greatest treasures!
SPIRIT. For one who is good in heart.
PRINCE. I am. Good and kind.

SPIRIT. As master of the palace you will appear to others as you are in your heart...

PRINCE. Then I shall appear as I always do.

SPIRIT. Until you can be loved for yourself.

PAGE. Your Highness...

PRINCE. Quiet! As master of such a palace I'll have little need for love!

SPIRIT. Your wish is granted. *(Music rises as SPIRIT vanishes, and gradually, on the distant hill, we see the palace very much like a rising jewel.)*

PRINCE. My palace! *(There is a shriek of wind, thunder and lightning. The music builds. As PRINCE steps toward the palace, he suddenly stops, screams and falls to the ground. PAGE backs off, terrified. He wriggles his hands and frees them. PRINCE can be heard groaning. PAGE approaches him and slowly kneels down.)*

PAGE. Your Highness, what's wrong? *(He reaches down to touch PRINCE, then gasps and backs away. PRINCE, behind a log or stump, gets to his hands and knees. His cries are animal-like.)* The Prince...the Prince is a beast! *(PAGE runs out. Lights dim. From behind the stump or log, PRINCE extends his arm which bears the claws of an animal.)*

CURTAIN

ACT TWO

SCENE: *Six months later. Morning. The exterior of the cottage where the family now lives. It is simple but charming, like a "big doll's house." BEAUTY is sitting on a bench near the door, sewing a patch on a pair of trousers, but at rise we can only see SPIRIT through the scrim and hear her music. Then she speaks.*

SPIRIT *(intoning)*. The days go by...one by one...the flowers bloom and fade...and bloom again...like our dreams...dreams come true...dreams come true...*(The lights change to reveal BEAUTY and the cottage as SPIRIT vanishes.)*

BEAUTY *(intoning with SPIRIT)*. Dreams come true... dreams come true...*(A little pause. She seems to awaken.)* Tell the truth, I'm not quite sure what my dreams really are. I mean, I love this place, all mixed up the way it is with trees and flowers and birds. And I love helping my family. *(Smiles.)* They seem to be growing up a little, too, and having fun doing it. *(Reflects.)* But I can't help feeling there's something missing, something I'm waiting for. What was it Toot Sweet said? "You're so busy being a broody mother hen you sometimes forget you've got dreams of your own." Maybe he's right. But what are they, Spirit, do you know?

(PAUL sticks his head out the window.)

PAUL. Finished patching my trousers?

BEAUTY *(back to earth)*. Almost.

PAUL. Rush not, Beauty, I haven't had a rest in months.

BEAUTY. You've really worked hard. Both you and Henri.

PAUL. Can you believe it? Me out there in the fields! Pretending I know what I'm doing?

BEAUTY. We'll be well supplied with food for the whole winter. You've worked miracles. *(Little pause.)*

PAUL. Beauty?

BEAUTY. Yes?

PAUL. I think I want to show you something.

BEAUTY. Really?

PAUL. Not much of a something, except that I made it!

BEAUTY. You did! What is it? *(PAUL hums a little, smiling, teasing.)* Come on, tell me.

PAUL. We *are* getting curious.

BEAUTY. We are not going to finish patching your trousers if you don't tell me! *(They laugh.)*

(TOOT SWEET enters and sees PAUL at the window.)

TOOT SWEET. You're supposed to be helping your brother in the field.

PAUL. Without my trousers?

BEAUTY. In a jiffy.

PAUL. What with all the parties and balls we've been having I'll need several new outfits. Think you can manage it?

BEAUTY. Mi'lord, for you I can manage anything.

Act II   BEAUTY AND THE BEAST   Page 23

TOOT SWEET. Here comes the one who does the managing.

(PAULETTE enters, checking her list.)

PAULETTE. Let's see. Noon. Almost. So—beds made, dishes done, garden weeded, field plowed, extra wood cut for stove. *(She spots them.)* This is no rest period. Paul, yonder fields beckon.

BEAUTY *(shows his pants)*. He needs these.

PAULETTE. No excuse. We stick to my schedule or else. Toot Sweet!

TOOT SWEET. More wood for the fire. Yes, mi'lady. *(He smiles and takes a few steps toward an exit.)*

PAULETTE. Where's little miss sweet-tooth?

BEAUTY. About somewhere.

PAULETTE. I'll check her nook inside.

PAUL. Paulette! Please!

PAULETTE. There's work to be done! *(Goes in cottage, PAUL gasps and ducks out of sight.)*

TOOT SWEET. What a change!

(BEAUTY nods and smiles. PAULETTE looks out the door and clears her throat.)

PAULETTE and TOOT SWEET. More wood for the fire. *(He exits.)*

PAULETTE. Our little sugar plum is not in her nook and it's time to start lunch. I see trouble ahead.

BEAUTY. I hope she hasn't wandered near that strange palace. *(Calling.)* Paul! You can dress for the party now.

(PAUL appears at the window and takes trousers.)

PAUL. Many thanks. Some sisters are kind and loving. Others, truth to tell, are...

PAULETTE *(grabs the trousers and moves away)*. Others are what? *(Small pause.)*

PAUL. Efficient. Terribly efficient. *(PAULETTE laughs and tosses him the trousers, and he disappears inside with them.)*

PAULETTE. Beauty?

BEAUTY. Yes?

PAULETTE *(looks around first)*. What would you say if I told you I'd made something rather nice?

BEAUTY. I'd say I want to see what it is!

PAULETTE. It wasn't easy. Not with my tight schedule. But I did it.

BEAUTY. What is it?

PAULETTE. You'll see. First, I'll make sure Henri is slaving in the field. *(Calling.)* Paul! You don't have to primp to plow. *(She marches off, checking list.)*

(TOOT SWEET enters other side with a bit of kindling. He nearly collides with PAUL as PAUL comes out and TOOT SWEET goes in the cottage. PAUL runs off and runs right back on and as he passes BEAUTY he says:)

PAUL. Don't move an inch.

(He continues to run off in back of the cottage. The second he's out of sight PAULETTE comes back in at a clip.)

PAULETTE. All alone?

BEAUTY. For the moment.

(PAULETTE, continuing the fast clip, starts for the house. TOOT SWEET comes out, picks up her pace and they both say:)

PAULETTE and TOOT SWEET. More wood for the fire!
(PAULETTE continues into the house, TOOT SWEET hides beside the cottage to watch.)
BEAUTY. My. My. My. *(Starts gathering up her sewing.)*

(PAULETTE comes out wearing an astounding hat. It is the picnic basket, now decorated with fruit and flowers.)

PAULETTE. Just take a look at this!
BEAUTY. Paulette! I don't believe my eyes.
PAULETTE. It *is* lovely. Would you believe I made it myself?
BEAUTY. No.
PAULETTE. Don't tell the others. They'd be so jealous. Want to try it on?
BEAUTY. If you'll let me.
PAULETTE. Here we go. I think it expresses a rather reckless mood, don't you?
BEAUTY. Is this right?
PAULETTE. Not quite. It's backwards.
BEAUTY. Now, do I look like a princess, or what?
PAULETTE. Either a princess or a moving garden! *(They laugh, then hear someone.)* It's Paul! Quick!

(PAULETTE takes the hat and goes in the cottage, just as PAUL comes around the cottage carrying a homemade birdcage which has a certain style to it.)

PAUL. Cast your pretty eyes on this, little girl.

BEAUTY. Paul! You're a genius!

PAUL. Yes, I know. The purpose, of course, is to house two song birds to serenade you while you work. Turtledoves, perhaps. I want to keep the help happy.

BEAUTY. I'm enchanted.

PAUL. Not a word to the others yet. Henri will turn green with envy. So will Paulette, which will be a big improvement.

HENRI *(calling off)*. Paul! Hurry up! It's your turn to be the horse.

PAUL *(calling back)*. Right away, dear brother. *(To BEAUTY.)* Our secret?

BEAUTY. Yes, dear brother! *(PAUL exits in back of cottage. BEAUTY and TOOT SWEET exchange smiles.)*

(HENRI enters from field.)

HENRI. Where is he? I simply can't push and pull the plow at the same time. Not for long I can't.

BEAUTY. He'll be there soon.

HENRI. You mean you're alone? Stay put. I'll be right back! And wait'll you see! *(HENRI exits.)*

TOOT SWEET. Not *another* secret!

BEAUTY. They're piling up, aren't they?

TOOT SWEET. Like dreams come true?

SPIRIT *(voice and music only. BEAUTY hears)*. Dreams come true...

BEAUTY. Like dreams come true. The Spirit was right.

TOOT SWEET. You wait, Beauty. One day the Spirit will send you a handsome young prince.

BEAUTY. I'll wait!

Act II   BEAUTY AND THE BEAST   Page 27

(HENRI enters carrying a bizarre female scarecrow.)

HENRI. Beauty, is this something or is this something!

BEAUTY. Henri! Did you really make it?

HENRI. Of course, and the only problem I can see, it's so marvelous it might attract the crows instead of scaring them.

BEAUTY. I see what you mean.

HENRI *(places the scarecrow at a little distance, very carefully, for BEAUTY's approval).* She's even better at a slight distance. More realistic. I started off modeling her after Paulette, so she'd be real scary, but she's turned out rather cute.

BEAUTY. I wouldn't tell Paulette.

HENRI. I'd jump in the well first. *(They hear PAUL, and they run to hide, joining TOOT SWEET, ALL giving each other the "Shh!" sign.)*

(PAUL comes from in back of the cottage and stops dead when he sees the scarecrow.)

PAUL. I've seen it all. *(Approaches the scarecrow.)* For one wild moment I didn't recognize you! Fancy!

(PAULETTE comes out of the cottage. PAUL, sensing this, studies the scarecrow and PAULETTE watches him. PAUL leans toward the scarecrow and gets "sincere.")

PAUL. Paulette, changing dressmakers was the smartest thing you ever did. You've never looked better. I mean it, Paulette. *(PAULETTE has taken a broom from near the door and is advancing.)* I can just see you now, dancing in the pig sty. *(He warbles.)* "Dance in the pig sty with me tonight..."

(POPPA appears at the window and watches.)

PAULETTE. I'll pig sty you! *(She goes after him with the broom.)*

PAUL. Careful, Paulette, I've just had my trousers patched. *(He uses the scarecrow as a shield.)*

PAULETTE. You'll need your head patched when I get through.

HENRI *(intercepting and taking the scarecrow)*. Don't you dare harm my scarecrow!

PAULETTE. Your what?

HENRI. Scarecrow. As in scaring crows. I made it myself. All you two can do is make trouble.

PAULETTE. Is that so! Wait'll you see. *(She goes into the cottage.)*

PAUL. I've made something that'll put that tacky stick doll to shame. *(He goes in back of the cottage.)*

POPPA *(from window)*. Are we having a contest?

BEAUTY. And you're the judge, Poppa!

(HENRI is clutching his scarecrow as PAULETTE sweeps out with the hat and PAUL runs back with the cage. At first they look with dismay at each other's creations, then guffaw and then start enjoying the whole thing.)

POPPA *(from window)*. Bravo! Superb!

TOOT SWEET. What talent! What artistry!

BEAUTY. And who wins the contest, Poppa? Can you ever decide?

Act II   BEAUTY AND THE BEAST   Page 29

(They change to mock beauty-contest entrants, parading about, posing. POPPA comes out of the cottage, climbs on the bench to watch. They begin to kid each other, finally trading props, PAUL wearing the hat, HENRI "chirping" with the cage, and PAULETTE dancing with the scarecrow and singing "Dance with me in the pig sty tonight, tra la!" HENRIETTE enters during all this and stops to watch.)

POPPA. Ladies and gentlepeople! *(BEAUTY runs into the cottage.)* We are pleased to announce the winners at this our first Festival of Frivolity. *(Cheers, applause, etc.)* For best hat, best birdcage. Best...uh...scarecrow? *(ALL nod.)* And best all-round nonsense, *my family* wins, hands down!

(Great cheers and BEAUTY comes back out with a small tray of sweets.)

BEAUTY. Here we go! Your prizes! Guaranteed to spoil your lunch!

HENRIETTE *(as the celebration continues)*. Oh, my goodness! I almost forgot to tell you! I have a surprise! No, I have two surprises.

BEAUTY. What are they?

HENRIETTE. A letter for Poppa! I passed the messenger way back at the river. He let me bring it. *(Takes the letter out of her apron pocket and gives it to POPPA who sits on the bench and starts to open the seal.)* I hope it's good news. Oh, and here's my other surprise. *(She looks back and motions, smiling.)* Come on! It's all right! *(To them.)* I found a friend, but he's shy, very shy.

(They watch as PAGE, looking tattered, enters. He stops and stares, then looks down.)

HENRIETTE. Don't worry, they won't bite.

POPPA. Who is it, Henriette?

HENRIETTE. Some poor boy who's been living in the forest all alone for months now. I found him near the river, fishing. He was hungry so I gave him my berry pudding.

PAULETTE. Your berry pudding?

HENRIETTE. You know, the berries I'd gathered, all smashed together.

PAULETTE (wincing). Nice.

BEAUTY. Alone in the forest? Don't you have a family?

PAGE. No. Not anymore.

HENRIETTE. We can be his family, can't we? That's what I told him.

POPPA. Good girl. We don't have much, but we're certainly willing to share.

PAUL. I'll even share the plowing, if you like.

PAGE. I want to help.

PAUL. Splendid.

PAGE. I'll do everything I can.

HENRIETTE. That's my poppa. And this is my sister, Beauty, only she's more like a mother.

POPPA *(who has been half listening, half reading)*. Listen! Listen to this! There's a chance, a very good chance that one of our ships was saved and lies safe in a foreign port. My old partner wants me to come right away and help identify the papers that have turned up.

BEAUTY. Right away?

POPPA. The sooner the better. If I leave now, I might be able to reach the city by sunset.

Act II   BEAUTY AND THE BEAST   Page 31

PAGE. You can be there long before that. I know a short-cut and I can guide you.

TOOT SWEET. Not near that strange palace!

PAGE. You'd never catch me there.

PAULETTE. Poppa, if it's true, we'll be rich again!

POPPA. Let's not count on it, Paulette.

PAUL. Oh, let's do.

PAULETTE. And start making lists of all the things we want.

PAUL. I'll get your coat. *(Starts in the cottage.)*

PAULETTE. And your scarf. *(She follows.)*

HENRI. And your hat. *(He goes.)*

HENRIETTE. I'll fix a lunch. *(She goes.)*

BEAUTY *(to PAGE)*. You take good care of my poppa.

PAGE. I promise.

TOOT SWEET. And bring him back as soon as you can. Stay clear of that palace.

(They come scrambling out of the cottage as they give POPPA his hat, coat and scarf and small packaged lunch. We glimpse a hooded figure, the BEAST, to one side. He is unnoticed and soon disappears.)

HENRIETTE. If you pass a candy store, maybe a few bon-bons...

PAULETTE. And some silk for a new dress...

PAUL. A few shirts with lace at the cuffs...

HENRI. Maybe shoes with silver buckles...

POPPA. I promise, I'll do my best. And for you Toot Sweet, a carriage with six horses? Would that do?

TOOT SWEET. No, eight horses. All white, please.

POPPA. Done.

PAULETTE. Don't tease, Poppa.

POPPA. All right, all right. I'll try to keep it straight. Some silk bon-bons, shoes with lace cuffs...Beauty, what's on your list? A handsome young prince? If I see one in a shop? *(The spirit music is heard briefly only by BEAUTY.)*

HENRIETTE. Yes, that's what she's always dreamed of.

BEAUTY. Or a rose, whichever you come on first.

PAULETTE. Mustn't dilly-dally.

POPPA *(as he gives little hugs and kisses and straightens his hat and scarf)*. Right you are, Paulette. Mustn't dilly-dally. Time to hop, skip and jump! *(They laugh and say good-byes as POPPA and PAGE exit. After the waves are over, BEAUTY drifts toward TOOT SWEET and the OTHERS look at each other smiling, then they burst out laughing.)*

PAULETTE. By the time Poppa gets back I'm going to have a list of things I want at least a mile long! I'd better get started! *(She goes in cottage.)*

HENRIETTE. Me, too! *(In she goes.)*

PAUL. Come on, Henri, before she uses up all the paper! *(They follow. TOOT SWEET and BEAUTY pause. BEAUTY goes and picks up the broom and turns back to look at TOOT SWEET.)*

BEAUTY. Poppa will never find anything as nice as these.

TOOT SWEET. Don't worry. They know that. They're just all aflutter for the moment.

PAULETTE *(off)*. Toot Sweet! Paul took my quill!

PAUL *(off)*. She took all the paper!

TOOT SWEET *(calls in)*. There's not one thing you need you don't already have. *(To BEAUTY.)* Right?

BEAUTY. Right.

Act II   BEAUTY AND THE BEAST   Page 33

(A rise in the bickering draws TOOT SWEET in, but he looks out the window.)

TOOT SWEET *(with a twinkle)*. Except maybe a handsome young prince. *(BEAUTY pretends annoyance and jokingly swings the broom in his direction as he laughs and vanishes.)*

BEAUTY *(revealing a secret to herself)*. A handsome young prince...wouldn't that be nice.

PAULETTE *(off)*. Beauty! *(Comes to the door.)* You've got to help me.

BEAUTY. Do what?

PAULETTE *(off)*. Strangle Paul.

(PAUL appears at the window, quill in his teeth, thumbs in ears and wiggling fingers.)

PAULETTE *(off)*. You give me that quill!

(PAULETTE chases PAUL into the cottage interior. BEAUTY shrugs and follows them in. The lights begin to dim. A little bickering can be heard. Suddenly the BEAST appears again. Very stealthily he approaches the cottage, his movements animal-like. He crouches for a moment beneath the window, then slowly, his back to us, he stands and looks in. He raises his arm up to lean on the top of the window and we now see the claws. A noise from inside the cottage causes him to back off, knocking over the scarecrow as he does. He turns and dashes off. Beat. TOOT SWEET comes out, having heard the scarecrow fall. He looks around, picks it up. As he does, BEAUTY appears in the door.)

BEAUTY *(half-serious)*. Toot Sweet, once they stop needing a mother, what will I be?

TOOT SWEET. Yourself, hopefully.

BEAUTY. Oh. *(Sees him looking around.)* What's wrong?

TOOT SWEET. Thought I heard something. Probably just your prince passing by.

BEAUTY. Come to serenade me at the window no doubt. *(They smile and pose as eerie music rises and the lights fade on them and rise on the palace in the distance.)*

CURTAIN

ACT THREE

SCENE: *The interior of BEAST's palace. It is beautiful, though at the moment only a glow from the fireplace casts any light, plus an occasional flash of lightning from the storm raging outside. A door to the outside is open—blowing open and shut in the wind if possible. After a moment we hear voices outside.*

PAGE. Please, we can't go in there!
POPPA. I must rest.
PAGE. Not in there. It's too dangerous.
POPPA. I'm not frightened. Come along.

(They appear outside the door.)

PAGE. I know who lives here. You must come away. Now. Before it's too late.
POPPA. No harm will come to us. *(Calling.)* Hello? Is anyone there? We seek shelter from the storm. Hello?
PAGE. He's hiding.
POPPA. You're imagining things.
PAGE. I told you. He's a beast. I saw it happen.
POPPA. No stories, please. I'm too exhausted. The door's open, see?
PAGE. It isn't a story, it's true.
POPPA *(starting in)*. We'll rest for a moment, then be on our way, once the storm lets up.

PAGE. I promised we'd stay away from this place.
POPPA *(inside)*. Help me find a chair.

(PAGE enters, takes POPPA's arm. They slowly cross to a chair and POPPA sinks down, a great sigh of relief.)

POPPA. There. Just for a moment.
PAGE *(now a frightened whisper)*. He's here—see, there's been a fire.
POPPA *(almost too weak to speak)*. There's no reason in the world for him to harm us.
PAGE. He doesn't need a reason. *(PAGE goes to a table and finds a candle. When his back is turned we see a shadow come and go. PAGE takes the candle and manages to light it from the embers, showing us a bit more of the room.)* You mustn't go to sleep.
POPPA. I'll just rest. *(PAGE explores a bit. He puts the candle on a table. He tries to tuck POPPA's coat around him.)*
PAGE. You should take off that wet coat. *(POPPA is asleep and doesn't answer.)* Asleep already. Poor man. Bad news in the city and now this. I'll stand guard. *(But his voice is shaky.)*

(PAGE reacts to thunder and lightning. Moves about a little, staying close to POPPA. In a moment, BEAST enters, unseen by PAGE. He moves from one spot to another, hiding where possible, until he is close to the candle. Quickly he extinguishes it, but before PAGE can call out, BEAST is upon him and they grapple. We hear only the muffled voice of PAGE, now gagged. The tussle continues as BEAST drags PAGE offstage.)

Act III   BEAUTY AND THE BEAST   Page 37

POPPA *(only half awake).* I must have dozed off. Don't worry, we'll only rest a moment...just for a mom...*(He sleeps.)*

(Pause. BEAST enters again. This time he goes to the outside door, slowly, pulls it shut and locks it. He crouches near POPPA and listens. He then sits in a chair with his back to POPPA and to us. Gradually the storm subsides, and the lights begin to show signs of dawn. In a moment there is more light. The back of BEAST's chair is high enough to hide all but the top of his head. A rooster crows. Soon POPPA stirs. He has slept but does not seem rested. He looks around.)

POPPA. Boy? Where are you? *(He does not see BEAST.)* The sun's coming up. We'd best be on our way. *(He starts to rise, stiffly, and looking very unhappy.)*

BEAST. Stay where you are!

POPPA *(startled, sinks back).* Who speaks?

BEAST. I do! *(POPPA looks around, then spots the chair.)*

POPPA. Forgive me for...intruding...

BEAST. Why should I? This is my palace! I do not open its doors to strangers.

POPPA. I'm very sorry. But the boy and I...where is he? The boy?

BEAST. He's gone.

POPPA. Gone? *(POPPA starts to rise again.)*

BEAST. I told you to stay where you are. I am master of this palace and you will obey me. *(He holds up a mirror for POPPA to see.)* My mirror! I can see you. And me.

POPPA. I hope no harm has come to the boy.

BEAST. He was once in my service. Before. Now he's gone to do my bidding.

POPPA. But he's come to live with us.

BEAST. With you and your family. I know. He's taken a message to them.

POPPA. I must go, too. What message? *(He rises and moves toward BEAST. A growling noise is heard.)* I thank you for giving me shelter from the storm last night, but now it's time for me to take my leave…*(He reaches a point where he can now see BEAST.)* No! *(He gasps loudly and the growl becomes a roar. POPPA runs in panic toward the outside door.)*

BEAST *(jumping from his chair his arms up to mask his face, but claws and mane showing, rushes after him).* The door is locked, foolish man! *(POPPA, near fainting, sinks back in the chair. BEAST goes back and forth in front of him, his back to the audience. We can see POPPA's frightened reaction.)* You are not leaving, not yet. Are you frightened? Look! Look in the mirror and see your face! See your frightened face! *(He laughs.)* What frightens you? *My* face? *(He looks at himself.)* Listen, old man. Your visit here will soon end. The sooner the better. We'll wait together. Which one will it be? Which daughter?

POPPA. What?

BEAST. I've sent the page with a message. You have three daughters.

POPPA. Yes.

BEAST. I want one of them.

POPPA. One of my daughters!

BEAST. Yes, one of them must take your place in my palace.

POPPA. I won't allow it!

Act III   BEAUTY AND THE BEAST   Page 39

BEAST. Or your family will never see you again.
POPPA. I won't allow it, I tell you.
BEAST. *You* won't allow it? *I* am master here!
POPPA *(calling)*. Help! Someone help me!
BEAST *(laughing)*. You're a fool. There's no one in the palace but me. I am alone, but not for long. *(POPPA suddenly makes a dash for the outside door again but BEAST quickly follows.)* I told you it's locked! *(POPPA moves away from the door.)* It's locked now, but we'll soon open it, won't we? Yes, we'll open it and welcome one of your daughters to my beautiful palace! *(He turns, laughing, waving the mirror, and for the first time we really see him. He is indeed a beast.)*

SCENE TWO

SCENE: *Again, the interior of the palace. The same day, several hours later, toward evening. POPPA is alone. He paces, looks out the window, tries the locked outside door. He goes to the mantle, checks the clock, then approaches the other interior exits but backs off, wary. He wipes his brow with a handkerchief, smoothes his coat hanging over a chair, then turns away, his shoulders shaking. There is a knock at the outside door. POPPA straightens, looks about and heads toward the door. The knock comes again. BEAST bounds into the room from an interior entrance. POPPA backs away from him.*

BEAST. Here. The key to the puzzle. *(He tosses POPPA a key.)* Aren't you curious?

POPPA. No harm must come to her. Give me your promise.
BEAST. If I did, would you believe me?
POPPA. I...I...would...
BEAST. Open the door.

(POPPA unlocks the door. BEAST gets the mirror and sits in the high-back chair. PAGE is outside.)

PAGE. Are you all right?
POPPA. Yes. Did you return alone?
PAGE. No. She wouldn't let me.

(PAGE steps aside and BEAUTY enters.)

BEAUTY. Oh, Poppa! *(They embrace.)* You're sure you're all right?
POPPA. Yes. But you can't stay here.
BEAUTY. I know what I must do.
BEAST *(who is watching in his mirror).* Stand aside, old man, so I can see her. *(BEAUTY, frightened by the voice, clutches POPPA.)* Stand by yourself. *Do as I say!* *(She moves a step away from POPPA, still holding his hand.)* Which one is it? Which daughter, you old fool. Surely you remember.
POPPA. Her name is Beauty.
BEAUTY. And my father is not a fool.
POPPA. Shh!
BEAST. Boy!
PAGE. Yes. *(Beat.)* Your Highness?
BEAST. Since you have obeyed me for once, you shall be rewarded. You're free. Free to leave with the old fool.
POPPA. I can't do it, Beauty. I just can't do it.

Act III   BEAUTY AND THE BEAST   Page 41

BEAST. You know what my demand is? *(Pause.)* Answer me...Beauty!

BEAUTY. The boy told me. I'm to take my father's place in your palace.

BEAST. Yes. You do this willingly?

BEAUTY. Willingly.

POPPA. Oh, Beauty.

BEAUTY. I can only be brave if you are. Besides, my lady will watch over me.

BEAST. Beauty and I wish to be alone, don't we, Beauty? *Don't we, Beauty?* Get out! Leave us! Or must I use force? *(PAGE spots POPPA's coat and gets it. They help him into it. As they do BEAUTY whispers something to PAGE and he nods.)* No secrets! No secrets from me!

BEAUTY. I...uh...want the boy to take good care of my poppa.

BEAST. Let the two fools take care of each other!

BEAUTY. Poppa, it doesn't matter that no ship was saved. We don't need a fortune, but we still need you.

BEAST. Out! Begone! Now! Before I throw you out! *(As PAGE urges POPPA out, POPPA touches BEAUTY's face and she smiles. The door is closed.)* Lock it. And bring me the key. *(Screaming.)* Did you hear me?

BEAUTY *(quietly).* Yes, I heard you. *(She locks the door and starts across the room. He watches in his mirror. She falters halfway then goes almost to his chair. With the mirror in one hand he suddenly thrusts out the other for the key. She reacts involuntarily, seeing his claw. Then she puts the key in it.)* There. Your key.

BEAST. Curious?

BEAUTY. What?

BEAST. Surely you're curious. And frightened. What does he look like? Can he be as awful as the boy said? As awful as he sounds? Look! Claws instead of hands! Why do you suppose he uses that mirror? *(Slowly he rises, and she backs off. Then he turns and stares. He bellows and waves his arms.)* Look at me! *(He waits but she is silent. He thrusts the mirror in her direction.)* Look at you! *(She hesitates, then in a moment she backs away and takes off her cape. She is trying to mask her fear.)*

BEAUTY. Is there a closet? *(BEAST points to archway or exit. BEAUTY takes her cape and hangs it up, then returns.)*

BEAST. Frightened?

BEAUTY. What are my duties?

BEAST. Your duties?

BEAUTY. Yes, you wanted me here. What am I to do? Is there a list of duties?

BEAST *(taken aback)*. First of all...

BEAUTY. First of all?

BEAST *(shouting)*. First of all...I command you to... smile! *(He looks in his mirror.)*

BEAUTY. I am to smile?

BEAST. You now dwell in the world's most beautiful palace. Is that not reason enough to smile?

BEAUTY. The palace *is* beautiful.

BEAST. I said it was.

BEAUTY. But, to smile...perhaps in time...

BEAST. *Now!* I am the master here! You will do my bidding.

BEAUTY. I will smile as soon as possible. I promise.

BEAST. Hang your promise. *(Pushes the mirror at her.)* Here. Smile at yourself.

Act III   BEAUTY AND THE BEAST   Page 43

BEAUTY *(turning her head).* What else? What else must I do?

BEAST. While I wait for your smile? Well, *(He goes to mantel.)* you'll make certain this clock is wound every fourteen days. Understand?

BEAUTY. Every fourteen days.

BEAST. Without fail. Starting now. Remember, I am master of this palace! Here! *(He forces her to take mirror.)* After you wind the clock, practice smiling! *(He races out. She waits a moment. Then she gets some paper from her cape pocket. She goes and finds a quill on a table.)*

(BEAST bounds back in.)

BEAUTY *(hiding paper).* Yes, sir?

BEAST. The key. For the clock. Keep it with you. *(He tosses it on the floor. She goes and picks it up, the mirror in her other hand, turns and walks to the mantel.)*

BEAUTY. Every fourteen days?

BEAST. That's what I said.

BEAUTY. Yes. That seems simple enough. *(She looks in the mirror.)* Smiles, I fear, won't come as easily. *(He grunts and exits. She begins to wind. Sound effect of clock.)* Every fourteen days...*(The lights dim down, until only the clock is glowing. And voice of SPIRIT is heard.)*

SPIRIT *(voice).* Fourteen days...like blossoms falling from a tree...a clock's ticking...and I watch and I wait...

(The lights are restored. Daylight. BEAUTY is writing at a table, occasionally glancing up to make certain she is alone.)

BEAUTY. "...you mustn't worry. No harm has come to me. I can't believe that another fourteen days have gone by. How I miss you. When I think of you, I try to smile." *(She folds up the letter.)* Now, it's up to the boy again. *(She goes and slips the letter under the outside door.)* There. I pray the boy never gets caught. *(She returns and walks about the room, now accustomed to its treasures. First she checks the clock.)* Almost time.

(She stops by a table and picks up a music box. After a slight hesitation, she opens the lid, and it plays. She puts it down and begins to sway and move a bit. The BEAST enters behind her, stops and watches. Then he tries to imitate her, but he is clumsy and stumbles. She turns.)

BEAUTY. I thought I was alone.
BEAST *(running out)*. You are!
BEAUTY. Come back, please!

(BEAST enters.)

BEAST. Why?
BEAUTY. Lovely, isn't it?
BEAST. That music box happens to be the world's finest, and it belongs to me.
BEAUTY. I know.
BEAST. Which means *I* say when it will be played. Is that clear? *(She closes the lid.)* Tend to your duties. *(He turns to go, but she speaks.)*
BEAUTY. Yes, I will. In a few moments another two weeks will have passed and I'll wind the clock.
BEAST. Did you...smile much at home?

Act III   BEAUTY AND THE BEAST   Page 45

BEAUTY. All the time. *(Catches herself.)* I mean, my brothers and sisters were always playing pranks...One time they...

BEAST. I've heard enough about your family.

BEAUTY. I talk about them because I miss them.

BEAST. What a pity.

BEAUTY *(going back to the music box).* May I?

BEAST *(grunts approval. When she looks doubtful he shouts).* Go ahead! Permission granted! *(BEAUTY starts the music, moves a little, then holds out her hands to him. She is still frightened in this scene so smiling is not possible. He slowly goes to her and thrusts out his claws. She takes them and tries to lead him in a simple dance, but he falters and nearly trips himself. Involuntarily she laughs, then gasps nervously.)* Don't you dare laugh at me!

BEAUTY *(fearful).* I didn't mean to. Really. I'm sorry.

BEAST. Not if you value your life!

BEAUTY. I won't do it again. I promise.

BEAST. You lie. I'm a beast and I'm clumsy and you find that amusing.

BEAUTY *(gently).* No one gets the hang of it the first time. Won't you try again?

BEAST *(yells).* Tend to your duties! *(He races out. She stops the music box, goes to the clock and starts winding. Sound effect. Lights dim down to the glow of the clock.)*

BEAUTY. Every fourteen days...

SPIRIT *(voice).* Every fourteen days...time slips by...and I watch and I wait...dreams come true...if you look in your heart...

(The lights are restored and the stage is empty. BEAST comes in, makes certain he is alone, then lifts the lid of the music box. He listens. He moves a paw in rhythm. He bows to an imaginary partner. BEAUTY enters behind him with a tray of food. She quietly puts it on a table, then turns to watch. BEAST starts to dance with his "partner" and he is not quite as clumsy. As he makes a turn he sees BEAUTY, stops center. Pause. She smiles, walks to him and curtsies. He bows, and they dance. When they stop again center, they separate a little.)

BEAST. No one gets the hang of it the first time. *(BEAUTY smiles again.)* A real smile.
BEAUTY. Yes.
BEAST. Because it's your duty?
BEAUTY. No.
BEAST. Your first smile. We should celebrate.
BEAUTY. We will. Look what I have. A little supper. *(She goes to pick up the tray and he picks up the mirror. He raises it slowly, almost afraid to look. She watches. When he sees himself he groans sadly.)* What is it?
BEAST. I thought I would change. When someone smiled at me, I mean. The mirror says "No."
BEAUTY. The mirror is wrong. Here. Supper for two. Pull the chairs up. High time we shared a meal together. *(BEAST's elation has gone and he merely grunts.)* Let's see. You sit there.
BEAST. I give the orders.
BEAUTY. Then order us to sit, I'm starved. *(BEAST, getting angrier, grabs a bowl and drops to the floor and begins to slurp like an animal. She watches, then takes*

Act III   BEAUTY AND THE BEAST   Page 47

the other bowl and joins him on the floor and tries to follow his example.) I need more practice. *(BEAST gets up, puts his bowl on table. He helps her to a chair. She waits for him to pull it out. He does. With a growl he plops down opposite her.)*

BEAST. Satisfied?

BEAUTY. This is my poppa's favorite dinner. "A good stew," he says, "may not look so appetizing, but just wait till you taste it." *(BEAST grunts, following her napkin routine, not too anxious to please, when it seems right, he makes it wrong.)* Paulette used to adore fancier dishes, but she's coming around. Doesn't even hold her finger out like this anymore. Dear Henriette, well, if it's sweet she's happy. *(He tries to follow her use of the utensils and deliberately errs.)* Paul feels that style in dining is everything, so poor Henri suffers. "Pull in your elbows, Henri, before a draft carries you aloft." *(BEAST sticks his elbows out.)* These days, though, with all the plowing they do, it's the size of the portion that counts. I've often caught them sneaking things off each other's plate. *(She jokingly reaches over to show him what she means. His reaction is automatic. He violently pushes her utensil aside, snarling.)* I was...only...trying to be...

BEAST *(ashamed, but still angry)*. I'm not one of your brothers. *(He gets up and goes to the exit.)*

BEAUTY. Wait. Our celebration isn't over.

BEAST. The mirror didn't lie. I'm still the same. *(He goes out. She thinks for a moment, then she starts with determination to follow him, but midway changes her mind. She straightens up the dinner things, then gets paper from the pocket in her cape and sits to write. She does so, silently, for a moment.)*

BEAUTY. "...of course it's not like home, but I do feel more comfortable as time goes by. But I ache to see you. Someday. Meanwhile, I'll dream of each and every one of you...love..." *(She looks up, not writing now.)* What was it Toot Sweet said? "You wait, Beauty, one day the Spirit will send you a handsome young prince." *(She smiles and folds the letter.)* I'll wait. And dream. *(Cautiously she goes and slips it under the outer door.)* We're lucky, he never uses this door.

(BEAST enters and sees her at door.)

BEAST. Thinking of leaving?
BEAUTY *(wary)*. The door's locked, remember?
BEAST *(snarl)*. Of course I remember. I've got the key, right here. *(He pats pocket.)* I've something else, too.
BEAUTY. What?
BEAST *(going to her)*. This. *(He offers a narrow box.)*
BEAUTY. Something for me? *(He grunts. She takes and opens the box and gasps.)* Oh, my goodness! *(As she holds up a string of pearls.)* I've never seen anything so lovely.
BEAST. You're pleased?
BEAUTY. With a string of tiny white blossoms? Almost like stars? Of course I'm pleased. Hold up your mirror. *(He does. She uses it to put the necklace on properly.)* But why?
BEAST. I didn't mean to spoil our celebration.
BEAUTY *(touches the mirror)*. You should throw this away.
BEAST *(stands beside her, holding the mirror in front of her and looking at her reflection)*. You're so...I'm try-

ing...I...Beauty, could you...ever love me? Even though I'm...*(He falters.)*

BEAUTY *(surprised, really).* Could...love you? I...I don't know. I mean we've become friends...I...*(She pushes the mirror down and faces him.)* It's so much easier for me, living here, than it was at first.

BEAST. You seem to smile quite a bit.

BEAUTY. Yes, I know. But to love someone takes more than a smile. Let's try to be even better friends, shall we? I want so much to please you. *(He looks in the mirror and turns to the exit.)*

BEAST. Good night, Beauty.

BEAUTY *(tries to think of something to say, can't).* Good night. *(He goes. She stands fingering the necklace.)* Once, I wandered off to gather flowers...I was hoping to find the prettiest blossoms in the world. I went further and further...and then I found them...here. *(She puts the necklace against her cheek.)* A string of tiny white blossoms...*(Still a little dazed she moves to the mantel.)* Oh, it's time. Every fourteen days...

SPIRIT *(as the lights dim down to the clock's glow).* Every fourteen days...see what's in your heart...see where you are...look at your dream...dreams come true...

(The lights are restored. BEAST is seated and BEAUTY is combing his mane. He pretends not to like it.)

BEAUTY. All right, now guess. Who's this? *(She imitates PAULETTE, not unkindly.)* "I don't give a fig how we do it just so we do it my way."

BEAST. Me.

BEAUTY. Well, you're close. It's Paulette! Toot Sweet once said her bite's worse than her bark.

BEAST. Me, too. Ouch!

BEAUTY. Come on. Try...I'll do another one. *(Imitation of HENRIETTE.)* "Did you know they invented sugar-plums just for me? Did you?"

BEAST. Paul.

BEAUTY. You're not trying!

BEAST. Be sure and comb the ends. Who's this: "My mane is the silkiest in the kingdom. Probably the world."

BEAUTY. Poppa.

BEAST. Ouch!

BEAUTY. If you're tired of my family...

BEAST. Bored silly. Ouch! That hurt!

BEAUTY. Well, hold still. Stop wriggling.

BEAST. Listen...

TOGETHER. I give the orders around here.

BEAST. Well, I do.

BEAUTY. I noticed.

BEAST. It does feel like silk, doesn't it? Or maybe spun air.

BEAUTY. Spun air?

BEAST. I'll take first prize at the festival. Easily. You'll see. I can hear the judges: "A matchless mane!" I might sell little strands for souvenirs. Want one?

BEAUTY. Yes, roots and all. *(Pulls.)*

BEAST. Ow! *(She dashes away laughing.)*

BEAUTY. Careful now. You'll muss that lovely mane.

BEAST. You know what I do with little girls like you? I eat 'em for dinner. Yum. Yum. *(They're running back and forth.)* But I'll spare you this time.

BEAUTY. Is there no end to your goodness?

BEAST. If you brush me for another hour or so, gently. *(Sits down.)*

Act III   BEAUTY AND THE BEAST   Page 51

BEAUTY. I quit. *(Tosses the brush.)* I'll find work at another palace. *(He goes to get brush, and she hides in an arch or behind a drape. When he looks around he starts searching, counting and looking for her at the same time.)*
BEAST. One...two...three...four...five...
BEAUTY *(jumping out)*. You're counting too fast again. Listen to the clock. Tick-tock, tick-tock. Just count on the tocks.
BEAST. My turn.
BEAUTY. Your turn!
BEAST. Hide your eyes.
BEAUTY. It's always your turn.
BEAST. Listen...
TOGETHER. I'm the master of this palace!
BEAUTY *(hiding her eyes)*. Honestly. *(Slight pause as he hides.)* I'll find you before "six." *(She starts counting and looking.)* One...two...three...four...five...six...
BEAST *(muffled)*. Seven ho-ho. *(BEAUTY stops and laughs and he sneaks up behind her and gives her hair a little tug.)*
BEAUTY. Ouch!
BEAST *(suddenly serious)*. I didn't scratch you, did I?
BEAUTY. I'm wounded! Alas! My smelling salts! *(She swoons and he awkwardly catches her and puts her "to rights.")*
BEAST. Sometimes I almost forget. *(Looks at claws.)*
BEAUTY. My family should see me. They just wouldn't believe it.
BEAST. Playing games?
BEAUTY. They'd probably send for a doctor, or faint maybe. Paulette would. Paul might find it all too amusing.

BEAST. You like acting a little foolish?

BEAUTY. Yes. I was always so...I don't know...serious. Very obliging, but sort of serious.

BEAST. I never acted childish before either. I was always so...serious. I was also mean and selfish and spoiled and vastly superior to anyone else.

BEAUTY. Perfect children.

BEAST. All right. Time to change games. Find the present.

BEAUTY. Not another present!

BEAST. Clues: it's small and round and begins with "r." And that's it. Ready?

BEAUTY. Are you going to hum?

BEAST. I'd rather growl.

BEAUTY. So you'll hum.

BEAST. I'll hum. *(As she begins to search for the present, he hums, softly when she's cold and loudly when she's warm)*

BEAUTY. What's that tune called?

BEAST. Small and round and "r."

BEAUTY *(repeats this as she looks)*. Rope?

BEAST. Nope. *(More humming.)*

BEAUTY. Wait! I know! Round and small and "r." A rose! Is it? I haven't seen a flower since I've been here. And roses are my favorite. Did you just guess?

BEAST *(has stopped humming)*. It's not a rose.

BEAUTY. Doesn't matter. Really. *(An idea hits her.)* Begins with "r"? *(He nods.)* It's a ring, isn't it?

BEAST *(getting box from mantel and speaking hesitantly)*. You're right. It *is* a ring. Here. And...it's...I guess you'd say...special.

BEAUTY *(sees it)*. Indeed it is! *(Starts to try it on.)*

Act III BEAUTY AND THE BEAST Page 53

BEAST. Wait. I don't think you're supposed to put it on yourself.
BEAUTY *(now she knows).* This ring means something, doesn't it? It's more than just a gift.
BEAST. Yes.
BEAUTY. You said it was special.
BEAST. Too special?
BEAUTY. I...I don't know. It's beautiful, but a wedding ring...*(Little pause.)*
BEAST. You don't have to say anything. I'll put it back.
BEAUTY. We've become such good friends, yet...
BEAST. There's something else. Something I've kept from you.
BEAUTY. Oh?
BEAST. This. *(Shows the key.)* I told your father it was the key to the puzzle. It's for that door. I'll leave it here, next to the ring...if...
BEAUTY. Please don't be upset.
BEAST. I should have known you'd prefer a rose. *(A pause, then he exits.)*
BEAUTY. Don't go. *(But he has. She goes and looks at the gifts, perplexed.)* The key to the puzzle. *(She takes the key and starts for the door and stops, staring off in his direction, struggling to make up her mind. Slowly she fetches her cape, puts it on and returns to the mantel where she looks at the ring again and puts it down. Then she unlocks the door and exits, leaving it slightly ajar.)*

(The lights begin to fade as BEAST re-enters. He stops and looks around. He goes about the room discovering her cape missing, the key gone and the door open. He

rushes to look outside and returns, crestfallen. Then he picks up the ring.)

BEAST. Round and small and begins with "r"...*(He puts it back. As he heads for his high-back chair he begins to break down. When he reaches the chair he sinks down on the floor beside the chair, weeping.)*

(The lights slowly fade until we see only SPIRIT through a scrim, perhaps above the mantel. During this short scene, BEAST actor discards his BEAST half-mask, claws, etc., or the scene could be taped audio, with SPIRIT mouthing. [In the original production the "tapestry" over the mantel was a scrim].)

SPIRIT. ...a realm of air and trees and flowers...a kingdom of space and beauty...you must remember...
BEAST *(voice)*. Ah, yes, all too well.
SPIRIT. ...a palace...a palace unmatched anywhere...rising like a great jewel...you must remember...
BEAST. As master of the palace...
SPIRIT. You will appear to others as you are in your heart ...until...until...
BEAST. I can be loved for myself.
SPIRIT. ...loved for yourself...
BEAST. My wish turned into a curse...
SPIRIT. ...you are certain...
BEAST. Before...before I thought I had everything...
SPIRIT. Before...
BEAST. Before Beauty. And now I have nothing. I am not loved for myself...I have nothing...
SPIRIT. If you dream a dream...
BEAST. Beauty did...she dreamed of her freedom...

Act III   BEAUTY AND THE BEAST   Page 55

SPIRIT. Dreams come true...

BEAST. And her dream did come true...she's gone...

SPIRIT. And I watch and I wait...*(The lights are restored. SPIRIT vanishes. BEAST lies beside the chair, partially out of sight. Pause.)*

(PAGE appears at the door. He carries a packet of letters. He looks in, then calls back softly.)

PAGE. There's no one here.

(BEAUTY enters cautiously. She doesn't see BEAST. She motions and the whole FAMILY appears in and around the door. BEAUTY gives them a "Sh" sign.)

BEAUTY *(in stage whisper)*. Stay close by. *(They nod and tiptoe away. To PAGE.)* Are those what I think they are?

PAGE. Yes, your letters. The ones I found and delivered.

BEAUTY. Oh, the clock! *(She goes to mantel.)* Just in time! *(She winds. Sound effect. No light change.)* Every fourteen days...

PAGE. Fourteen days?

BEAUTY. Yes, I've never missed. I promised.

PAGE. Has he really changed?

BEAUTY. Yes. Don't be frightened. *(A moan from BEAST.)* Listen!

PAGE. Look! Over there! *(She rushes to BEAST and kneels.)*

BEAUTY. What's happened? Please, can you hear me?

BEAST. I thought you'd gone forever.

BEAUTY. No, just to fetch my family. It took longer than I thought. I want them to meet you. I want them to know you.

BEAST. No, send them away.

BEAUTY. What did the Spirit tell you when you wished for the palace?

BEAST. It doesn't matter.

BEAUTY. Not to me, perhaps, but I realize how much it means to you.

PAGE. She said he'd have to be loved for himself. I was there. I heard it.

BEAUTY. Can you get up or are you too weak? Please try.

BEAST. It's no use.

(BEAUTY motions for PAGE to summon the OTHERS. He does, and they quietly come in and form a group on one side, ALL very curious.)

BEAUTY *(gets the ring from the mantel and goes back to BEAST)*. I think you're supposed to help me with this, so you'll just have to get up. *(Pause.)* Shall I start counting to see how long it takes? Or what? *(He rises and turns so we ALL see. It is the PRINCE. A pause as they look at each other. She smiles, gives him the ring and he slips it on her finger. Applause and "oohs" and "aahs" from the OTHERS.)*

PAULETTE. The gifts!

HENRI. We forgot the gifts!

PAUL. No, we didn't forget them, we were just waiting for the right moment. Which is now! *(They rush out.)*

HENRIETTE *(as they go)*. Don't anyone eat my gift! *(Over her shoulder as she exits.)* We follow Paul's list these days! Imagine! *(POPPA and TOOT SWEET stand near the happy COUPLE.)*

(SPIRIT appears, watching.)

POPPA. Additions to your collection of treasures.

TOOT SWEET. Made by some truly gifted artists and awfully nice people.

(HENRIETTE runs in first with a wooden bowl.)

HENRIETTE. Some of my famous berry pudding for the wedding feast! *(The OTHERS bring on the things they made earlier—the hat, the cage and the scarecrow—all now bedecked with bows and ribbons.)*

PAGE *(offering the letters)*. Here, Your Highness. You can read all about how she fell in love with you.

PRINCE *(takes mirror and holds it to look at BEAUTY's reflection)*. I can read that here. *(She smiles, takes the mirror and gives it to PAGE.)*

BEAUTY. We don't need this anymore. *(POPPA gives the PRINCE a rose and he passes it to BEAUTY.)*

SPIRIT *(as the music rises)*. Dreams come true...dreams come true...

CURTAIN—END

DIRECTOR'S NOTES

DIRECTOR'S NOTES

DIRECTOR'S NOTES

DIRECTOR'S NOTES

DIRECTOR'S NOTES

DIRECTOR'S NOTES

DIRECTOR'S NOTES